CW01023335

SURFING IN BRITAIN

FOURTH EDITION

? Luke Hendy,
wan slash.
'AGE: Huge
reak. Photos:
earle.

Published by Orca Publications Ltd, 11 Cliff Road, Newquay, CORNWALL TR7 2NE (tel: 01637 878074). Edited by Chris Power. Production by Mike Searle, Louise Webb and Steve England. Colour Repro by Picture House. Printed by Rowe the Printer. Distributed by Orca Publications Ltd (tel: 01637 878074). Copyright c MDCCCCLXXXXV Orca Publications Ltd. All rights reserved. No part of this publication may be reproduced in any form (including by electronic means) without written permission from the publishers. Reproduction without permission is a breach of Copyright Law and will result in prosecution. While every care has been taken in producing this publication, the publishers assume no responsibility for affects arising therefrom.

INTRODUCTION

Foreword

by Colin Wilson, British Surfing Association administrator and development officer

Welcome to the fourth edition of THE guide to surfing in Britain. This new edition contains nearly twice as much information as the previous one, including new sections about equipment, surfing technique, how to predict swells, and what to do in an emergency.

There really is something for everyone in this book, whether you're an absolute beginner or a competition-standard surfer. More than 180 of the best surf spots in the country are listed, and the information is up-to-date and accurate.

This guide has been produced on behalf of the British Surfing Association which is the governing body for surfing in Britain. BSA members receive many benefits including our bi-monthly magazine Surf News, free public liability insurance, free advice about any aspect of surfing, and discounts at many surf shops.

If you would like to find out more about the BSA, please write to us at the following address: British Surfing Association, Champions Yard, Penzance, Cornwall TR18 2TA.

Good surfing!

Some history

Surfing was introduced to Britain in the 1960's by travelling Australian lifeguards who had come over to find summer jobs patrolling beaches in Cornwall. They bought with them their Malibu boards (similiar to today's longboards), and were soon enjoying the chilly but uncrowded Atlantic waves.

The local's, impressed by what they saw, soon wanted boards of their own, and the demand prompted Newquay craftsman Bill Bailey to build the first British boards under the label Bilbo.

Soon surfing competitions were being held, and in 1966 the British Surfing Association was formed.

A year later Britain's Rodney Sumpter (who'd grown up in Australia) won the World Junior Title, and became an instant celebrity.

The '70s saw rapid developments in surfing equipment. Shorter boards gave rise to a new form of 'radical' surfing, with the emphasis on manoeuvres.

In the '80s, events like the Fosters and Hot Tuna Surfmasters at Fistral Beach, Newquay, attracted the world's top pro's, among them British-born Martin Potter (who won the World Title in 1989).

Home-grown talent flourished in the late '80s and early '90s, with Paul Russell, Carwyn Williams, Spencer Hargraves, and Russell Winter in turn dominating British and European competitive surfing.

Today, tens of thousands of people enjoy riding waves in Britain. And there's still no better way to escape the pressures of the world for a few hours than by going surfing.

Clean, offshore conditions at a west Cornwall beachbreak. Photo: Mike Searle

7

Advice for beginners

Surfing is a challenging sport to master, but once you're 'up and riding' you'll see that it's brilliant fun. If you want to learn to surf you must be a good swimmer, and be fit. Good eyesight is also important; many surfers with poor vision overcome the problem by wearing soft contact lenses (and keeping their eyes firmly shut underwater).

Just as novice skiiers spend their first days on the slopes at ski school, so novice surfers are strongly advised to spend their first sessions at a surf school. Being taught the correct techniques by a properly-qualified instructor is inexpensive and can save you hours of frustration. And learning about safety precautions is of paramount importance: the ocean is a dangerous place to play if you don't know what you're doing. For a list of surf schools approved by the British Surfing Association, see page 12.

Besides the basic surfing techniques you'll be taught at a surf school, you'll also come across a number of important do's and don't, which apply to all surfers:

DO observe restricted-area flags, and warning flags: a zone with black-and-white chequered flags is a lifeguard-supervised area for beginner surfers; a zone with yellow-and-red flags is a swimmers-only area. If a red flag is flying, the beach is closed to swimmers and

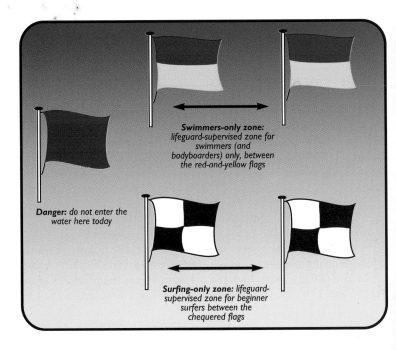

Swimmers-only zone: lifeguard-supervised zone for swimmers (and bodyboarders) only, between the red-and-yellow flags

Danger: do not enter the water here today

Surfing-only zone: lifeguard-supervised zone for beginner surfers between the chequered flags

When you wipeout, try to fall off behind your board and push it away from you. Photo: Chris Power.

beginner surfers because conditions are unsafe; experienced surfers who paddle-out in such conditions do so at their own risk.

DO stick a nose-guard onto the tip of your board, and blunt the trailing edges of your fins if they're sharp.

DON'T surf alone.

DON'T go surfing straight after a meal, or after drinking alcohol.

DON'T 'drop-in' on another surfer. The surfer nearest the curl of the wave has right-of-way.

DON'T bail your board when paddling out through waves if you can possibly help it, there may be someone right behind you.

Hazards

✗ Rip currents Water pushed towards a beach by the action of waves will flow back out to sea as a rip current. Rips can usually be identified from the shore as channels of deeper water (often between sandbanks) where the waves aren't breaking; the surface of the water may look rippled, or be discoloured by suspended sand. Although they're usually only a few yards wide, a rip current can quickly drag an inexperienced surfer out to sea. If you get caught in a rip, don't try to paddle back to shore straight against the current, but paddle across it to wherever the waves are breaking. Never leave your board, it's your life-raft. If you need help, wave your arms and shout to attract attention.

✗ Rocks If you're surfing a rocky reef or point break, wear a helmet and boots.

✗ Pollution Sadly, many of Britain's surfing beaches are affected by sewage or industrial pollution, because for decades the water companies responsible for coastal effluent disposal failed to tackle the problem. Cases of various illnesses have been attributed to surfing in polluted seawater, and in recent years the pressure-group Surfers Against Sewage (tel: 01872 553001), have been vocal in highlighting the issue.

Improvements are slowly being made to the sewage treatment works around Britain's coast, but some of the most popular surfing beaches may still have to wait until the next century for clean water. Beaches which fly the EC Blue Flag comply with European water quality standards.

✗ Weeverfish Despite their size (often only 6" long) the weeverfish can inflict an excruciatingly painful sting. Weevers are most likely to be encountered at low tide at sandy beaches during warm summer weather, when the fish come into shallow water to spawn. If stung, the affected limb should quickly be submersed in very hot water (as the venom is de-activated by heat) and pain-killers taken. Sting relief spray (such as Wasp-eze) can also help.

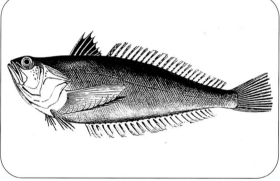

✗ Jellyfish Occasionally encountered on onshore days during the summer, jellyfish stings to exposed areas (usually the hands) can be painful, but your wetsuit will protect the rest of you.

You'll definitely know about it if you tread on one of these.

✗ UV radiation Even in Britain, intense summer sunshine can cause sunburn and the associated increased risk of skin cancer.

When on the beach, use a sunscreen cream or cover yourself up; when in the water, use a waterproof sunblock.

SURF SCHOOLS

The best way to learn how to surf, quickly and safely, is to go to a BSA-Approved Surf School. There are currently seventeen in Britain, so phone and find out where to join up from the list opposite.

With good tuition and guidance from professional instructors you will get the hang of surfing much sooner than if you were flapping around on your own in the white-water and progress much quicker. The courses are fun to go on, and many offer good 'Apres Surf' activities ranging from BBQs, to coastal boat cruises and surf video evenings.

What do they teach you?

Like any sport, you can't learn the more progressive manoeuvres until the basics are mastered. This takes time and practice. During the course your instructor will take you through all the relevant surfing techniques, safety tips and theory. The Welsh and British National Surfing Centres also have courses for the disabled and visually impaired.

Where can you do it?

On the following list you'll find details of all the BSA-Approved Surf Schools around the UK, which are all based in the South West and South Wales. The British Surfing Association set up the scheme in 1990 to help the public obtain better value-for-money and greater safety whilst being taught. The schools and ensure their instructors must adhere to guidelines laid down by the BSA to make sure that a high standard of coaching and safety is met.

Some surf schools also run BSA Fin Awards courses. These are proficiency tests aimed at assessing your surfing ability; they range from the Blue Fin award through to the Gold Fin award. To collect a Gold Fin you must be able to catch a green wave in at least 3ft of surf, ride along it and execute a controlled turn.

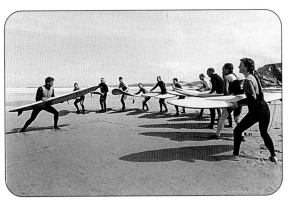

A BSA Instructor takes a lesson on Tolcarne Beach, Newquay.
Photo: Chris Power

1. Twr-Y-Felin Outdoor Centre
St Davids, Dyfed, SA62 6QS
Tel: 01437 720391
2. Haven Sports
Marine Road, Broad Haven, Dyfed,
Pembrokeshire, SA62 3JR.
Tel: 01437 781354
3. Welsh National Surfing Centre
87 Harding Close, Boverton
Llantwit Major, S. Wales.
Tel: 01446 793279
4. PGL Adventure
Beam House, Torrington
N. Devon, EX38 8JF. Tel: 01805 22992
5. Buckland Manor
First Raleigh, Bideford, N. Devon,
EX39 3NJ. Tel: 01409 281806
6. Woodside Adventure Centre
First Raleigh, Bideford, N. Devon,
EX39 3NJ. Tel: 01237 474496
7. St Georges House
Georgeham, N. Devon, EX33 1JN.
Tel: 01271 890755
8. Outdoor Adventure
Atlantic Court, Widemouth Bay
Bude, Cornwall, EX23 0DF.
Tel: 01288 361312
9. Surf's Up
Valley Caravan Park, Old Polzeath,

Cornwall, PL27 6SS. Tel: 01208 862003
10. National Surfing Centre
(at Fistral Beach, Newquay)
BSA Office, Champions Yard, Penzance,
Cornwall, TR18 2TA.
Tel: 01736 60250
11. Newquay Surfing Holidays
Box CA, 4 Beachfield Avenue,
Newquay, Cornwall. Tel: 01637 872756
12. Offshore Surfing
38 Pendragon Crescent, Newquay,
Cornwall, TR7 1SY. Tel: 01637 877083
13. Natural Balance Surf Co
14 Fore Street, St Ives, Cornwall,
TR26 1AB. Tel: 01736 793264
14. TJ's School of Surfing
1a The Meadow, St Ives, Cornwall
Tel: 01736 797348
15. Up & Riding Surf School
Riviere Sands Holiday Park, Hayle,
Cornwall. Tel: 01736 752132
16. Freetime Surf School
Runnelstone Cottages, St Levan,
Penzance, Cornwall, TR19 6LU.
Tel: 01736 871302
17. Sennen Surfing Centre
4 Trevilley Farm Cottages, Sennen,
Cornwall, TR19 7AH.
Tel: 01736 871458

EQUIPMENT

SURFBOARDS

There are three main types of surfboard – soft boards, 'pop-out' boards, and custom boards – all available in a range of sizes and shapes.

Soft surfboards are made from a semi-rigid plastic foam which is soft and very buoyant. They're ideal for first-time surfers, and are consequently widely used by surf schools. Once you've mastered the basics on a soft board you should move on to a more rigid pop-out or custom board which will be have much more drive. Soft surfboards cost around £150.

A pop-out (or moulded) surfboard is constructed by joining the two moulded-fibreglass halves of the board together, then filling the middle with liquid polyurethane foam which then hardens. Pop-outs are heavier than custom boards, but are harder wearing, so they're ideal for novice surfers who've done a few days' tuition at a surf school and want to move on. They cost £100 - £150.

Custom surfboards are made by hand from polyurethane foam 'blanks' which are shaped and then covered with a thin layer of fibreglass. These boards can be made to any shape or design required, with any colour scheme. They're lightweight, but easily damaged. Suitable for beginners and experts alike, custom boards cost £230 - £350.

If you're buying your first board, think volume. A big, high-volume board will be stable, easy to paddle, and catch a lot of waves. Generally, a beginner's board should be at least 12" longer than you are tall, and thick enough to provide plenty of buoyancy. Seek advice about what sort of board you should buy from a friend who surfs, or a reputable surf shop.

A secondhand board can be a good bet if it's suitable for you, and free of defects; a few dents in the deck are nothing to worry about, but delamination can be a real problem. Dings that have been properly fixed won't affect performance; but avoid snapped boards which have been "repaired as good-as-new" according to the salesman, as these are prone to snap again and the rocker may well be out of line. Again, seek advice from a friend who surfs before buying.

BODYBOARDS

Bodyboards are rectangular boards made of polyethelene which are designed for riding waves lying down ('prone') or on one knee ('drop-knee'). They cost £50 - £200.

Bodyboarding has now become a sport in its own right, with its own magazine THREESIXTY available from all good surf shops and newsagents in Britain. A comprehensive guidebook The THREESIXTY Bodyboard Manual, which tells you everything you want to know about bodyboarding, is also available price £2.95 (incl. p&p) from Orca Publications (tel: 01637 878074).

WETSUITS

A good wetsuit is a must for surfing in British waters. Wetsuits are made of neoprene rubber, and there are designs and thicknesses to suit all water temperatures and uses. A good all-round choice would be a full-suit (long arms and

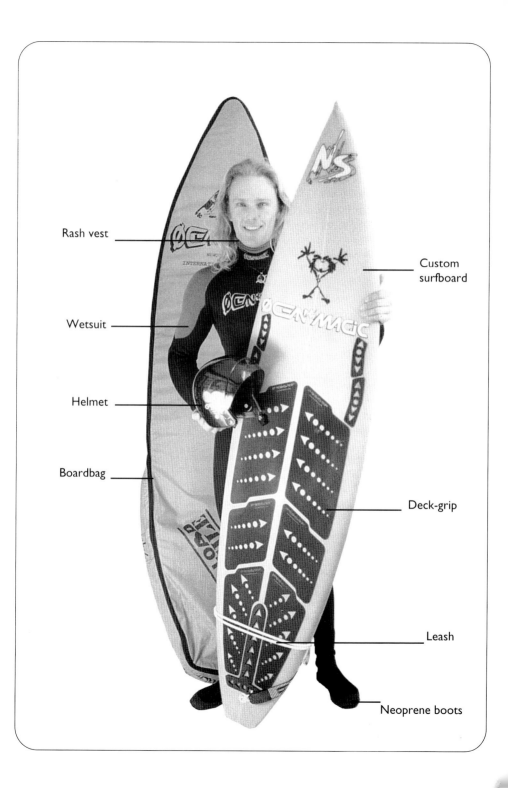

Rash vest

Custom
surfboard

Wetsuit

Helmet

Boardbag

Deck-grip

Leash

Neoprene boots

legs) with 4mm legs and lower body, and 3mm arms and upper body. Make sure the wetsuit fits snugly: there should be no baggy areas, and the legs and arms should be the right length. Unless you have an unusual body shape, you should be able to buy a suitable wetsuit off-the-peg. Custom-made wetsuits are also available. Wetsuits cost £80 - £220.

For added comfort, wear a lycra rash-vest under your wetsuit; this will prevent chaffing under the arms and around the neck.

Most British surfers wear neoprene boots, gloves, and hoods during the winter months.

ACCESSORIES

A leash is a stretchy cord (made of urethane) fixed to the tail of the surfboard, which straps onto the rear leg of the surfer. A leash should always be worn: it prevents you losing your board in the water,

and stops the board from hitting other surfers or bathers nearby. Leashes cost £12 - £20.

Fibreglass surfboards would be slippery to stand on if they didn't have some sort of grippy surface. Some surfers use deck-grip (a stick-on spongy material) which provides good traction but is expensive and cannot be re-used. Other surfers go for the traditional option, wax, which is cheap but needs to be re-applied each session. A full deckgrip kit costs around £45; wax is £1 a block.

A padded boardbag will protect your precious custom board from knocks and bangs. The best ones have 10mm high density foam padding, metal zips, and adjustable shoulder straps. Boardbags cost £50 - £80.

It's a good idea to wear a helmet if you surf shallow reef or point-break waves. The most popular brand made by Gath cost around £50.

ANATOMY OF A SURFBOARD

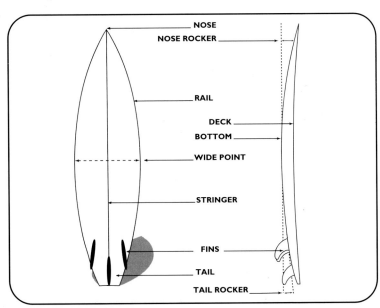

NOSE
NOSE ROCKER
RAIL
DECK
BOTTOM
WIDE POINT
STRINGER
FINS
TAIL
TAIL ROCKER

ASP top 44 Pro Jake Spooner ripping on a NS at Hossegor. Photo: Joli

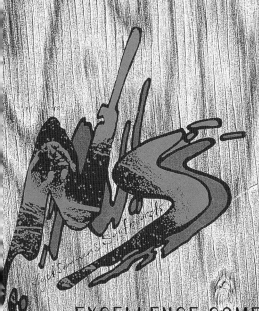

Pre-surf checks

Before going surfing always check out the conditions, and the state of your equipment.

Beginner surfers should only surf at beaches under the supervision of qualified lifeguards, and stay within the black-and-white chequered flags (see page 8).

Intermediate level surfers arriving at a beach should observe warning flags and notices, and ask the lifeguards' advice about where to surf and any hazards to be avoided. Spend at least ten minutes checking out the conditions. Are there any rips or rocks to stay clear of? Time the sets – how often are they coming through? Where are the other surfers getting in and out of the water? (If there are no other surfers out, there's probably a good reason – the waves could be heavier than they look, so go and check out another more sheltered spot instead.)

Next, check your equipment. Is your leash okay? There should be no nicks or kinks in it. Wax the deck of your board if necessary, and make sure your board has no unrepaired dings you could cut yourself on.

Finally, do some stretching exercises to loosen up your muscles. Cold, stiff muscles and ligaments can easily be wrenched and strained by a bad wipeout, but you can avoid this risk by spending five minutes warming up.

Paddling out

Wade out up to waist-deep water, holding your board out to one side of you (so it doesn't bash you when a line of whitewater comes through). Then jump up on your board, and lie on it centrally, so the board's nose is just clear of the surface of the wave. Keep your legs together and paddle using a swimming 'crawl' stroke. Keep your head up to see where you are going.

When a line of whitewater comes towards you, push yourself up off your board using your arms (as if you were doing a press-up), so the wave passes between you and the board. Hang on tight to the rails of the board because there'll be quite a bit of turbulence.

As you improve you'll find that the key to paddling out is to use a steady rhythm; don't paddle flat out, but go at a steady pace. Save some energy for the occasional burst of speed you'll need to get over a big incoming set.

Catching broken waves

Select an incoming whitewater wave that is about 10 metres away from where you are. Swing your board around so it's pointing at the beach, and adopt the paddling position. Make sure that no one else is already riding the wave, and that there's no-one in your way who you could collide into. When the wave is five metres away from you, start paddling as hard as you can; you'll need to do at least six or eight strokes to catch it. Keep glancing behind, so you know when the wave is about to reach you.

If you've timed it correctly you'll feel yourself lifted up and pushed forward by the wave.

Now comes the hard part: getting to your feet. Hold both rails of the board, with your hands positioned under your chest, and push yourself up into a standing position in one smooth movement. Keep your feet about two feet apart, and assume a crouched position. Stand with your back foot at 90 degrees to the board's stringer, and your front foot at 45 degrees. Look

Paddling out. Photo: Chris Power.

where you are going, not at your feet.

As you get the hang of it you'll find you to get to your feet quicker, and you'll then have time to steer your board a bit by leaning slightly in the direction you want to go.

Duck diving

Once you can ride broken waves with confidence you're ready to venture farther 'out the back' to the lineup. But to get there you have to get past bigger and bigger lines of whitewater, as well as unbroken waves; to do this you need to learn how to 'duck dive'.

Duck diving involves sinking your board right under the oncoming wave, then popping up the far side. By pushing your board deeper than the wave's zone of turbulence (usually only a couple of feet deep) you avoid getting dragged back towards the beach the whole time.

1. Paddle hard towards the oncoming wave, so you have some forward momentum.

2. Just before the wave reaches you, grab the rails of the board under your chest, lift your backside, and lean forwards straightening your arms as you do so; this will begin to sink the nose of the board. Now bring one of your knees up under your body, place it on the tail of the board, and shove the board down and forwards underwater. Take a deep breath as you do this.

3. If you've dived deep enough, you'll feel the wave going past above you. Once it has passed, your board's buoyancy will lift you quickly back to the surface. Lean backwards and you'll pop up even faster.

Most intermediate surfers find duck-diving the most strenuous aspect of going surfing, as it requires a fair bit of effort. If you find yourself struggling, build up your upper body strength between surf trips by doing regular exercises (especially push- ups and stomach curls).

Soft boards and pop-out boards are hard to duck-dive because of their large volumes; thinner custom boards are much easier.

Spencer Hargraves takes off on a clean reef-break wave in Lanzarote. Check out how quickly he's got to his feet, and how he's already started to turn his board along the wave by leaning slightly to the right. Photo: Martin Taylor.

Lee Bartlett turns hard off the bottom at a Cornish secret spot, leaning all his weight on his inside rail. Photo: Mike Searle.

Once you've mastered duck-diving using one knee, try bringing a leg up under your body and pushing with your foot on the tail of the board for deeper penetration.

Catching unbroken waves

So now you're 'out the back' and ready to catch some unbroken waves. Before paddling for a wave, spend a few minutes watching where the other surfers are taking off, and how the waves are breaking. Don't paddle for 'closeouts'; go for waves which are peeling. Remember to look both ways along a wave before paddling for it — another surfer may already be up and riding. **Remember the drop-in rule: the surfer nearest the curl has right of way**.

The technique is the same as that for catching broken waves except that you need to get to your feet quicker, and keep your balance as you take-off down the face of the wave, which will be quite steep. Lean forward, but not too far forward or you'll 'pearl' (dig the front of the nose)

Bottom turns

The first turn you make at the base of the wave is called the bottom turn. A good bottom turn will set your course along the wave, and transfer the speed from the take-off into down-the-line speed.

Advanced surfers steer smooth, wide bottom-turns and crouch down low so they can spring up into their first manoeuvre farther along the wave with the maximum possible momentum.

Wipeouts

If you feel yourself losing balance, wipeout safely by falling clear of your board, preferably behind it. Never dive off head-first in shallow water (unless you want to spend the rest of your life in a wheelchair). If there is a danger of your board hitting someone else, try to hold onto it.

After a wipeout, come up to the surface with your arms over your head, in case your board springs back on its leash unexpectedly.

SEC OND SKIN
SURFSUITS

EXETER ROAD • BRAUNTON
N.DEVON • EX33 2JL
Tel: 01271 813300

It's not the quality of the neoprene, the Titanium lining, the blindstitched seams, the heat taped stress points, the standard Melco flexible knee pads or the minimum seam/panel design that are the most important things to look for when choosing a new surfsuit. Warmth, comfort and durability all depend on FIT.

"There's no point buying the top name wettie with the latest gizmos if it's not a perfect fit."
Carve Magazine No.4 - wetsuit review.

After measuring over twenty seven thousand people I have yet to find a perfect standard sized person. Try measuring around your right arm and leg and compare with the left, nearly everyone will find a difference.

This is why all Second Skin surfsuits are made to measure (both sides) at no extra cost. They are even cut specifically for your sport.

Send off the coupon or phone for a free brochure, or even better still call in at our new surf shop in Braunton and check out our range, starting from only £75.50 for a full suit.

We also stock surfboards by Beach Beat, Nat Young, Local Motion and Second Skin. Bodyboards by Manta, Rheopaipo, Genesis and Wedge Warrior. Surfwear from Bear, Maui and Sons, Greg Noll, Local Motion, No Fear, Stussy and Second Skin.

PLEASE SEND A BROCHURE TO:

NAME:...

ADDRESS:...

....

MANOEUVRES

CUTBACKS

Cutbacks are basic, functional manoeuvres which enable the surfer to change direction and steer back to the 'pocket' (or curl) of the wave, where the most energy is.

A powerful cutback can be a highly satisfying manoeuvre in its own right. To carve a clean powerful arc at full-speed feels great, and you can throw up loads of spray.

The type of cutback you can perform depends on the kind of wave you're surfing, and the speed you're travelling. Slow, mushy waves will require small snappy cutbacks, as speed is lost very

quickly. In larger waves with more power the surfer can travel farther out onto the shoulder before cutting back. A 'roundhouse cutback' is where a surfer carves a big cutback right around, and then whacks his board off the lip of the pocket.

Step 1: You've ridden along the wave and are now up on the shoulder – the wave is less steep here and there's less energy, so it's time to cut back to the pocket. Initiate the turn by increasing the pressure on your outside rail, and turning your head and shoulders towards the shore.

Step 2: As you drop down the wave the board will accelerate, but maintain your course by fixing your sights on where you're going – the pocket. By turning your head and shoulders, you'll find your whole body will twist in the direction you want to go, and the turning force will be transferred to your board. Keep your knees bent and your

Tom Carroll gouges a heavy forehand cutback at Rocky Point in Hawaii. Notice how he turns his head and focusses on where he's heading – back towards the pocket. Sequence: Mike Searle

body low for stability.

Step 3: After you reach the bottom of the wave you'll start to decelerate, so ease the pressure off the rail (so it doesn't snag) and set up your next turn in front of the pocket. When completed, you'll be heading along the wave in the same direction as when you started, having followed an S-shaped course.

OFF-THE-TOP TURNS

The off-the-top (or off-the-lip) is another fairly basic manoeuvre, which can also be spectacular when performed at speed. By steering your board right up to the top of the wave, you'll be in a position to take the drop again and re-coup energy to accelerate off down-the-line.

A steep 'wall' section of the wave is the place to do an off-the-top.

Once you've mastered off-the-top turns you can start thinking about doing floaters and other lip tricks.

Step 1: Look for a fairly steep section of the wave and set up the manoeuvre by doing a big wide bottom turn: you'll need quite a bit of speed to get up to the top of the wave.

Step 2: Steer your board up the face of the wave, transferring your weight onto the tail of the board as you hit the lip. Turn your head and shoulders towards the beach at the same moment.

Step 3: As you complete the turn and start to drop down the wave face, try to stay centred on your board and keep low for stability.

The forehand off-the-top, as performed by Kelly Slater. By turning his shoulders anti-clockwise as he hits the lip (notice he's bringing his right arm forwards) he's setting up a turning force which will cause the board to pivot on its tail. Photo: Hank.

TUBE RIDING

Spencer Hargraves tucks into a beach-break tube at Hossegor in France. Riding frontside, notice how he's using his leading arm to point the way, while trailing the other to feel how close he is to the wave face. Photo: Pete Frieden.

Riding inside the tube of a wave is the ultimate surfing thrill. Surfers who've experienced a deep tube ride will happily witter on about how incredible it felt for hours. "You sort of get enveloped in energy," says Newquay's Daz Wright, "you see that green lip come over, and it's like you should be being totally crushed, but you're not because nothing's touching you."

Hollow, tubing waves occur when the swell is clean and fairly powerful, and only at certain spots – reef-breaks and shallow sandbar beachbreaks.

When the waves are six feet and barrelling, wave selection is all-important. "You want to pick a wave that looks really thick, like it's going to double-up," says Daz, or one that's got a bowl section on it, so it looks kind of a horseshoe shape."

The drop will be steep, but assuming you make it you can line yourself up and pull in. If you're riding frontside, you can stall your board to get deeper into the tube by putting all your weight on your back foot for a moment, and by sticking your 'inside' hand into the face of the wave. Once you're in the tube you need to accelerate to get out of it, so shift your weight forward, hopping quickly forward with both feet if necessary.

FLOATERS

The floater was the move of the '80s in the world of pro surfing, but it has now become a standard manoeuvre of any surfer's repertoire.

There are two basic types of floater, both of which involve manoeuvring your board up on top of the breaking lip, then free-falling back down with the curtain of the wave. The **section floater** is where the surfer floats over a breaking section, then continues on along the wave. A **floater re-entry** is where the surfer ends his ride with a floater as the whole wave closes out.

At contests, the floaters that score the highest marks are those where the surfer glides along the lip for as long as possible. "Speed is the name of the game," says British champ Randall Davies, "the faster you go, the longer you go."

The hardest part of doing floaters is committing yourself and steering your board out of the lip and towards the trough. "You've just got to be confident that you're going to make it from the start," says Randall, "because if you're thinking 'I'm going to fall' then nine times out of ten you will fall."

As you come down try to stay centred over your board, and bend your knees to cushion the impact as you land.

Californian pro Rob Machado pulls off a backhand floater at Seignosse in France. Look carefully and you can see that as well as dropping down the wave, he's also glided four or five yards along it by the time he lands. Sequence: Chris Power.

Taylor Knox jams a tail-slide on a beachbreak closeout: notice how he's put all his weight on his front foot, and has shoved the tail round by extending his back leg. Photo: Alex Williams.

TAIL-SLIDES
by Rob Small

The tail-slide is one of surfing's most radical small-wave manoeuvres. Performed at maximum speed, the surfer hurtles towards the lip and turns with so much power that the board breaks out of its forward track and slides around through 90 or even 180 degrees, before the fins re-connect and allow the surfer to continue his ride.

Advanced surfers can perform tail-slides in such critical positions that the whole tail of the board breaks free, leaving the area under the front foot as the only part of the board in contact with the wave.

Tail-slides are difficult manoeuvres to pull-off, but they're brilliant fun when you can do them. The sensation of being almost out of control as you drift sideways along the wave is one you don't forget quickly!

Beachbreaks with fairly powerful 2-4 foot waves (clean, or slightly crumbly) are perfect for tailslides. Bigger, down-the- line waves provide less opportunity, but innovators of tailslides such as Kelly Slater and Shane Powell still manage to pull them off regularly.

Step 1: Find a sucky section and get your board going as fast as you can. Keeping your back foot planted way back over the fins, do a hard bottom turn and aim for the lip as if you were going for an off-the-top, but travelling a little bit too fast.

Step 2: Hit the lip and simultaneously shift all your weight onto your front foot. If you have enough speed, this should allow the tail to break free and provide a pivot point around which the tail can slide – if you want to give an extra shove with your back foot, go for it!

Step 3: Once your board has slid around, centre your weight again and hang on. As soon as the fins bite into the wave, the board will automatically swing around and gather forward momentum. This will happen pretty suddenly and can catch you off guard, so stay crouched really low to maximise your chance of recovery.

REVERSES

The 'reverse' (reverse 360) is a tail-slide variation where the surfer slides the tail so far around that he's actually travelling backwards for a moment, then completes the manoeuvre by spinning the board all the way through 360 degrees. To pull one of these off you need to be going really fast, and have the agility and balance of Himalayan mountain goat.

As with tail-slides, the key to doing reverses is to shift all your weight forward onto the front foot (grab the front of your board with your hands if necessary), so the board's fins are out of the water while the board spins round. Keep your rear foot right on the tail for maximum leverage, and stay really low for stability.

In this tail-slide sequence Hawaii's Cory Lopez slides his tail so far around that he comes down the wave backwards. Sequence: Alex Williams.

AIRS

by Rob Small

An air (or aerial) is a manoeuvre where the surfer blasts off the top of the wave, turns his board in mid air, and lands it. Airs are among the hardest tricks to master, but they're guaranteed to get the adrenaline pumping. They also score highly at surf contests, being spectacular crowd pleasers.

Airs are generally performed in smallish waves, as there would be too much speed to control in larger conditions. Welsh pro Carwyn Williams suggests that "the ideal wave size would be anything between three and six feet". Sucky shorebreak waves are ideal.

The direction of the wind can also play a part; a light cross-shore can help you get maximum lift and height.

Step 1: Look for a sucky section and get your board going as fast as you can. Do a hard bottom turn, but don't go as wide as you would to set up a vertical off-the-top, so you can charge up the wave face at full speed. Keep your board 'flat' to the wave face, and stay slightly crouched so you can spring off the lip.

Step 2: As you hit the lip, unweight and give a small boost with your back foot (like doing an 'ollie' on a skateboard). This should throw you upwards and forwards. It is important at this stage to keep your weight centered over the board; some people grab a rail with one hand to help control the board.

Step 3: Landing is the most difficult part. You need to have flown with a trajectory that's taken you out in front of the wave, so that you land on the curtain of the wave (not the back of it). Keep your knees bent to absorb the impact, and hang on!

Airs are always tricky moves to pull-off successfully, and to land big ones you need a lot of commitment and a fair bit of luck. You can also damage your surfboard... and yourself. Carwyn cheerfully explains that "the things most likely to snap, if you're not careful, are your ankles!"

LONGBOARDING

Surfing took off as a sport in the '50s and '60s with the introduction of foam-and-fibreglass boards. These traditional-shape boards, around ten feet long, were the predecessors of today's modern longboards which although similar in length are lighter and more responsive.

Surfers who ride longboards tend to adopt a smoother, more style-orientated approach to wave riding than the cut-and-thrust of the shortboard fraternity. This is partly due to the physical restrictions of wielding a nine-foot board, and partly due to the the historical tradition of surfing gracefully.

Since 1986 longboarders have had their own professional World Championships; recent champions have included Nat Young, Joey Hawkins and Rusty Keaulana.

Because they're big and buoyant, longboards are easy to paddle and have a lot of stability. During the summer months when the waves are small, you can often have more fun cruising around on a longboard than you would on a low-volume shortboard.

Many of the basic surfing techniques already described also apply to longboards, but some are slightly different.

PADDLING OUT

There are two ways to paddle a longboard: lying down in the normal 'prone' position, or 'knee paddling' in a kneeling position which allows more powerful strokes.

Due to their size and volume, longboards can't be duck-dived under oncoming lines of whitewater; instead, paddle hard towards the wave, and shift your weight back over the tail just before the wave reaches you, so the nose lifts up over it. Alternatively, if an oncoming wave is about to land right on you, do an eskimo roll and hang onto the front of the board underwater.

BOTTOM TURNS

You can take-off much earlier on a longboard than you would on a

(Left) Today's longboarders can pull off many of the same manoeuvres as shortboarders. Nick Carter launches a floater at Fistral Beach. Photo: Mike Searle.

shortboard – even before the wave has started to pitch. By angling the take-off you avoid dropping straight down the face of the wave and the risk of pearling.

When you reach the bottom of the wave, step back on your board and lean gently in the direction you wish to take. Bear in mind that longboards are heavier and less responsive than shortboards, so don't lean so hard that you overbalance. As you come out of the turn, move forward on your board to bring it back into trim.

CUTBACKS

To cutback on a longboard you need to step right back and get your rear foot over the fin (or fins). Keep your knees bent and remember not to lean too far or too fast.

NOSE RIDING

Nose-riding, where the surfer walks up to the front of the board, is the ultimate traditional longboarding trick. The kind of waves best-suited to nose-riding are longish, steadily-peeling waves, the glassier the better. "Basically you do a bottom turn, set your line just a little bit high, and cross-step your way to the front of the board," says British number one Chris 'Guts' Griffiths. "Once you're actually on the nose, your weight will bring you back onto the line you would have taken if you were just riding along the wave normally. You need to be right in the curl, so there's whitewater breaking over the tail of the board. That balances the board, keeping the nose up."

How many times have woken up in a frenzy, fallen down the stairs, and screeched down the road to the beach... only to be confronted by ripples? It's a bummer.

But how can you predict when a swell is likely to arrive? Actually it's not all that hard, once you've learnt how to read weather maps.

Waves are caused by wind blowing over the surface of the ocean. The size and type of the waves generated depends on three factors: the wind speed; how long the wind blows in a constant direction; the 'fetch' (the distance that the wind blows over the water's surface in a constant direction).

If the wind is strong and blows for a long time, across a long distance in the direction of your beloved beach, then you should be in for plenty of swell!

Thanks to Michael Fish and his mates at the BBC, you can see detailed weather maps on the TV every day. Most quality newspapers also print useful maps, and you can even have a forecast chart faxed to you by the Met office by dialing 0336 400 445 (about £1.50 per fax).

Swell is generated by low pressures systems (storms) that constantly travel around the globe, moving from west to east. These 'lows' are shown on

(Above) Light offshore winds help make waves 'clean' and well-shaped. South Fistral. Photo: Chris Power. (Below) By studying weather maps like this MetFax, you can predict when and where a swell will hit.

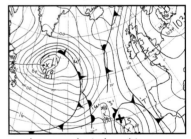

weather maps by isobars (air pressure contours) which indicate the wind direction and wind speed. In the northern hemisphere, winds always rotate anti-clockwise around lows. The closer the isobars, the stronger the wind.

High pressure systems (which usually bring settled, sunny weather) have winds which rotate around them in the opposite – clockwise – direction.

Looking at the weather chart shown above, we see an intense low pressure system situated out in the mid-Atlantic, with its centre measuring 969 millibars. As the isobars are packed tightly together, gale force winds will be howling around it, and blowing in a westerly direction around the underside of it; this will produce a big swell moving in a westerly direction.

Open ocean swells travel at 20-25 mph, and since the low is about 1000 miles away from Britain, the swell being generated will start to arrive in approximately two days' time.

Swells like this tend to fan out away from the generating wind direction, by perhaps 30 or 40 degrees. So this swell will provide waves for most of the west-facing coasts of Europe, from the Hebrides right down to the Canaries.

Our chart also shows an area of high pressure centred over Denmark. If this was to stay there for the next few days it would provide light southeasterly winds (remember, the winds follow the isobars and rotate clockwise around highs), which would blow offshore along the north coasts of Devon and Cornwall, giving classic surfing conditions.

Swells that are generated a long way out in the ocean, then travel for days before hitting land, will be well lined-up and 'clean' when they arrive (provided there's little or no wind when they do). These are called **groundswells**, and provide the best conditions for surfing.

Strong local onshore winds will also generate swell, but it will be of the messy and choppy variety, with the waves close together. This kind of swell is called a **storm-swell**, and the waves will be erratic and hard to ride.

DEVON & CORNWALL

The north coast of Devon and Cornwall is the most popular area for surfing in Britain. The Atlantic provides a steady supply of west swells, and outside of the summer months it's rare to see completely flat conditions. But although there's usually swell, offshore winds from the southeast or east are required for really classic conditions.

Along the south coast of the two counties there are a number of good spots which work on southwest swells generated by cyclonic depressions ('lows') out in the Bay of Biscay.

NORTH DEVON

1 Lynmouth Good left point break over boulders, at the mouth of the River Lyn. Only works on huge swells (usually in the winter) when beaches like Croyde are 6ft plus and maxed-out. Fast-breaking waves, best from low to mid-tide, pushing in. Light southerly winds blow offshore. Advanced surfers only. ✘ Rocks, submerged marker poles and other obstacles; pollution.

2 Woolacombe Popular, west-facing beachbreak, works at all stages of the tide. Needs a clean swell and easterly winds to be really good. **Coombesgate** (or Barricane) Beach, to the north, can offer good low-tide waves.

3 Putsborough Protected from south and southwest winds, this northwest-facing beachbreak works best from mid to high-tide.

4 Croyde Popular (can get very crowded) west-facing beachbreak, with sometimes excellent tubey waves at low tide. Unsuitable for beginners at low tide. ✘ Rips when over 3ft.

5 Downend Point Seldom-ridden right point-break, needs a clean 6-8ft swell; works around low tide. Advanced surfers only. ✘ Rocks, difficult access, rips.

6 Saunton West-facing beachbreak, with some protection from northerly winds; slowish waves (ideal for beginners).

7 Westward Ho! Average west-

facing beachbreak, works on all tides.

Also in this area:
Spot 'Z' Sheltered, north-facing left pointbreak which needs a massive swell to work. Fast and hollow waves,which break over cobblestones, best around high tide. Advanced surfers only.
✘ Rocks, marker poles and other obstacles; pollution.
Spot 'Y' Sheltered, north-facing spot with lefts breaking over sand-and-rocks along the side of an old collapsed rock breakwater. Only works on big swells, and on very low (spring) tides. ✘ Rocks.
Spot 'X' Remote, west-facing spot with good rights breaking over sand-and-rocks. Best on a clean 3-5ft swell, from low to mid-tide. Access via a bumpy track. ✘ Rocks.

BUDE AND NORTH CORNWALL

8 Duckpool, Sandymouth, Northcott   West-facing beachbreaks with scattered rocks,

A surfer races a fast left-hander at a beachbreak in west Cornwall
Photo: Mike Searle

hence usually surfed around low tide. Not suitable for beginners. ✘ Rips when over 3ft; rocks.

9 Bude This popular resort's two town beaches, **Crooklets** and **Summerleaze**, both face west and work on most tides. ✘ Rips at low tide when over 3ft.

10 Widemouth Bay Popular west-facing beachbreak; works from quarter-tide up, with waves often improving towards high tide.

11 Bossiney Haven Sheltered north-facing beachbreak; only works on a big swell, around low tide (submerged above mid tide).

12 Trebarwith Strand West-facing low-tide beachbreak (submerged above mid tide).

13 Polzeath Popular west-facing beachbreak, best on a clean swell with light south-easterlies. Works on all tides.

14 Harlyn Small, crescent-shaped bay which faces north. Can provide fun hollow waves (and quite a few close-outs) when a big swell is running and nearby beaches like Constantine are onshore and maxed-out. Best from low to mid-tide.

15 Constantine Bay West-facing beach with rocky outcrops at each end. Picks up any swell going, but is adversely affected by any wind other than from the east quadrant. The central stretch of beachbreak is best from mid to neap-high-tide. For advanced surfers, there's a low-tide righthander at the northern end of the beach (Booby's Bay) which can be good, and a mid-tide left at the southern end; both break over sand-and-

DEVON & CORNWALL

30.

31.

rocks. ✘ Rips when over 3ft, rocks.

16 Treyarnon Narrow west-facing beach, best around low tide. ✘ Rips when over 3ft.

Also in this area:
Spot 'W' Challenging left point, only works on big swells (usually in winter) and needs to be 6ft plus to break clear of the rocks. Holds waves up to 12ft, works around quarter-tide only. Fast, heavy wave for experts only. ✘✘ Rocks, rips.

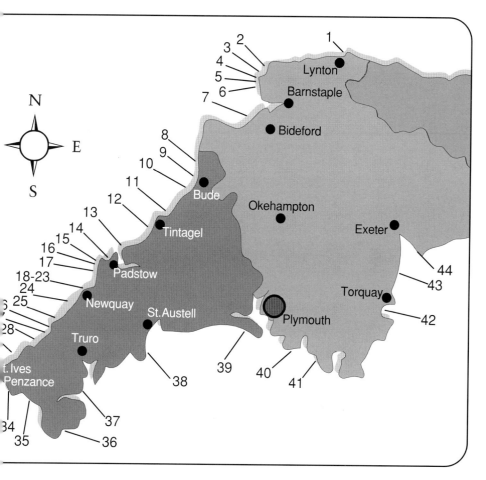

NEWQUAY AND THE MID-CORNWALL COAST

17 Mawgan Porth West-facing beachbreak, best from low to mid-tide.

18 Watergate Bay Popular west-facing beachbreak just north of Newquay, often crowded during the summer if the waves are good. Works on all tides (one of the few beaches in the area which is good around high tide). ✗ Rips over 4ft.

19 Whipsiderry Low to mid-tide beachbreak (submerged at high tide), partially sheltered from south-westerly winds.

20 Newquay Bay Newquay's three north-facing town beaches — **Tolcarne, Great Western** and **Towan** — join up at low tide to form a mile-long stretch of sand; at high tide they're submerged. Always popular, and often crowded during the summer, despite the fact that most of the waves are close-outs. Best around mid tide, with a light westerly cross-shore. **Tolcarne Wedge**, a high-tide cross-wave at the south end of the

A clean summer swell at Putsborough in North Devon.
Photo Chris Power

beach, is popular with bodyboarders. ✘ May occasionally be affected by sewage pollution from the outfall at nearby Towan Head.

21 Fistral Beach North-west facing beachbreak, works on all tides, with fast hollow waves at low tide under ideal conditions. Good rights along the north headland when the sandbars are lined up. Always crowded when good. Britain's most famous surfing beach, the venue of several major contests each year. ✘ Rips when over 4ft; may occasionally be affected by sewage pollution from the outfall at nearby Towan Head.

22 Crantock Low-tide sandbank at the southern end of the beach sometimes good on big swells (advanced surfers only). ✘ Rips.

23 Holywell Bay North-west facing beachbreak, best around three- quarters tide. ✘ Rips when over 4ft; parts of metal shipwreck exposed in middle of the beach at low tide.

24 Perranporth Two-mile stretch of west-facing beachbreak; cliffs at either end give some protection from cross-shore winds. Waves at the southern (**Droskyn**) end of the beach are predominantly slowish lefts, best around three-quarters tide. The middle stretch (**Perran Sands**) can be reached via the holiday camp on top of the dunes, and offers peaky waves, best from mid to neap-high-tide. **Penhale Corner**, at the northernmost end of the beach, can be a good low-tide right-hander when the sandbar is lined up. ✘ Rips when over 4ft; MoD firing range at the top of the cliffs

O 1 2 7 1 8 1 6 2 2 7

Fistral Surf Co

Truro Lanes, Kenwyn Street, Truro
01872 260850

19 Cliff Road, Newquay, Cornwall
01637 850378

1 Beacon Road, Newquay, Cornwall
01637 876169

THE LARGEST AND BEST SURFING RETAILERS IN EUROPE

CLOTHING
Instinct
Rusty
Body Glove
Hot Buttered
Gordon & Smith
Bear
Sex Wax
Kangaroo Poo
Tucano
Finch
Mystic Knights

WETSUITS
Sola   Victory
Gul   Hot Buttered
Body Glove   F.S.C

SHOES - Boks, Country Leather

FREE
FULL COLOUR
MAIL ORDER
CATALOGUE OUT
NOW

SEND S.A.E TO
CLIFF ROAD OR PHONE
OUR HOT LINE:-

01637 877687

SURFBOARDS
Rusty
Instinct
Bunty/Local Hero
Pottz
Hot Buttered
Gordon & Smith
Kamikaze
F.S.C
Second hand boards available

BODYBOARDS
Morey   Wave Rebel
BZ   Ocean & Earth
Rheopaipo   Hot Buttered
Custom X   Scott
Second hand boards available

SUNNIES - Bolle, Legend

at the northern end of the beach.

25 St Agnes North-facing beachbreak which works on big swells and is sheltered from westerly winds. Predominantly rights breaking away from the rocks in the middle of the cove; best around low tide on a small swell, or around mid tide when it's over 4ft. Always crowded when good. ✘ Past pollution problems should be eradicated by new treatment works due to be completed in 1996.

26 Chapel Porth West-facing low-tide beachbreak (submerged after mid-tide). ✘ Rips when over 3ft.

27 Porthtowan Northwest-facing beachbreak, works on all tides (one of the few beaches in the area which is good around high tide). ✘ Rips when over 3ft; occasionally affected by sewage pollution from outfalls to the west.

28 Portreath harbour wall Short wedgy right-hander breaking over rocks at high-tide; faces north and needs a big swell to work. Expert surfers only. ✘✘ Rocks; occasionally affected by sewage pollution from nearby outfalls.

Also in this area:
Spot 'V' Northwest-facing spot with rights and lefts breaking over sand-and-rock; works from low to mid-tide on biggish swells. Long walk down cliff path. ✘ Badly polluted area, rocks.

WEST CORNWALL

29 St Ives Bay Three miles of beachbreak stretching from Godrevy round to Hayle. At the northern end, **Red River** (or Godrevy) faces west and picks up any swell going; it works on all tides up to neap high, but will be affected by any winds other than from the east quadrant. **Gwithian**, the next spot along, works under similar conditions. ✘ Rips when over 4ft.

30 Porthmeor St Ives' main surf spot, a beachbreak which faces north and requires a biggish swell. Works on all tides, best from mid to high tide. Always crowded when good. ✖ Rips when over 4ft.

31 Sennen Cove West-facing beachbreak near Land's End, best around mid tide. **Gwenvor**, at the northern end, works best from low to mid-tide. ✖✖ Rips when over 3ft.

32 Porthcurno Small, southeast-facing cove, one of the few Cornish spots where winds from the northwest blow offshore. Works on a southwest (or big west) swell, only on very low (spring) tides. Marvellous scenery. Not suitable for beginners. ✖ Rips

33 Newlyn harbour wall Sheltered right-hander which faces southeast, and only breaks a couple of times a year on humongous swells. Long but slowish wave, best from mid to three-quarters tide. ✖ Rocks, submerged old cars and other obstacles.

Steve England in action at a mid-Cornwall beachbreak. Photo: Chris Power

THE SOUTH COAST OF DEVON AND CORNWALL

34 Praa Sands, Perranuthnoe Southwest-facing beachbreaks which work on southwest swells when the wind is from the north quadrant. Fast, sucky waves breaking close to the shore, best from mid to high-tide. Of the two beaches, Praa gets the more swell.

35 Porthleven Excellent right reefbreak, situated just west of the harbour entrance. Good barrels when it's on. Holds waves up to 12ft. Ideally needs a big west (or southwest) swell plus a northeasterly breeze; consequently it doesn't work very often. Best from mid to three-quarters tide (dangerously shallow at low tide); must be over 4ft to break clear of the rocks. The reef at the end of the harbour wall is sometimes good at low tide giving short, hollow lefts-and-rights; again, it's dangerously shallow. Experts only. Be considerate to local residents. ✘✘ Rocks; past pollution problems should be eradicated by new treatment works due to be completed by 1995.

36 Kennack Sands Southeast-facing beachbreak, best around mid tide. Works on big southwest swells, and on southeast swells.

37 Falmouth Two of the town's beaches, Maenporth and Gyllyngvase (which both face southeast) occasionally get surf after an easterly wind has been blowing along The Channel for a couple of days. Best from low to mid tide.

38 Pentewan Southeast-facing beachbreak, best around mid tide. Works on southeast or huge southwest swells.

39 Whitsand Bay Long southwest-facing beach offering average waves, best at low tide. ✘ Rips.

40 Wembury South-facing spot with waves breaking over sand and rocks. Best from low to mid-tide. ✘ Rocks.

41 Bantham Southwest-facing beachbreak at the mouth of the River Avon. Can offer good fast rights when it's on. Needs a big southwest swell plus winds from the east quadrant to work. Often best after a dry spell has caused the rivermouth sandbar to build up. Works on all tides. Often crowded when good because of its proximity to Plymouth. ✘ Rips when over 3ft.

42 Paignton East-facing beachbreak near the pier. Only works on short-lived east swells. Best from mid to high tide.

43 Teignmouth East-facing beachbreak, only works on short-lived east swells. Best around high tide.

44 Exmouth, Sidmouth Southeast-facing beachbreaks which only work on short-lived east swells. Best around high tide.

Also in this area:
Spot 'U' Southwest-facing lefthand reef-point, only works on big southwest swells; exposed spot, affected by any winds other than from the east quadrant. Best around high tide. Great scenery, abundant cabbages. ✘ Rocks.

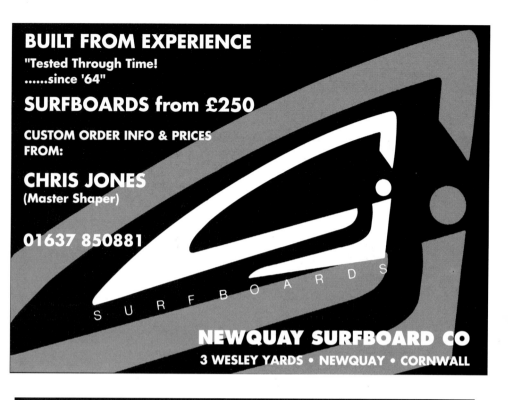

WALES

The south and west coasts of Wales have dozens of good breaks, which pick up west and southwest swells.

MID AND SOUTH GLAMORGAN (AND THE RIVER SEVERN)

1 The Severn Bore Tidal bore which travels up the River Severn and is rideable on spring tides. Best ridden on a longboard, the bore is usually caught at Minsterworth, and can sometimes be ridden for over a mile. For bore size predictions and times, phone the National Rivers Authority (Severn-Trent region) on 01684 850951. Not suitable for beginners. ✘ River currents; floating obstacles; thick mud.

2 Llantwit Major Right point-break over boulders. It faces south, needs a big swell, and only works from low to mid-tide. Advanced surfers only. ✘ Rocks; rips.

3 Southerndown Southwest-facing beachbreak, best from low to mid tide.

4 Ogmore-by-Sea Occasionally good lefts break into the rivermouth here, over a sand bottom. Faces southwest, and needs a big clean swell to be good; works from mid to neap-high-tide. Not suitable for beginners. ✘ Rips; pollution.

5 Porthcawl Point Right point-break, 3-6ft, situated at the western end of Sandy Bay. It faces south so needs a big swell to break, and glassy conditions (or light northerlies) to be any good. Works from mid to high-tide. Always crowded when good. Advanced surfers only. ✘ Rocks; rips.

6 Coney Beach Average south-facing beachbreak popular with Porthcawl's younger surfers when Rest Bay is big and onshore. ✘ Rips at the eastern end.

7 Rest Bay Exposed southwest-facing beachbreak, best around mid - tide.

8 Aberavon Wedgy peak that

breaks over a sand bottom next to the breakwater at the southern end of the beach. Long, hollow lefts and short rights when its good. Presently under threat because of port development plans. Faces west, so winds from the east quadrant blow offshore. Best around three-quarters tide. ✘✘ Pollution; rips.

THE GOWER PENINSULA

9 Crab Island Good right-hand reef break, 3-10ft, at the eastern end of Langland Bay. Only works around low tide. Always crowded when it's on. Needs a clean swell and glassy conditions (or light northerlies) to be any good. Advanced surfers only.

✘ Rocks; rips.
10 Langland Bay Popular (always crowded when good) south-facing bay with waves breaking over sand-and-rocks. Works on all tides. ✘ Rocks; rips when over 4ft.
11 Caswell Bay Popular south-facing beachbreak, best from mid to neap-high-tide.
12 Oxwich Bay Sheltered southeast-facing beachbreak with fun, hollow waves around neap-high-tide (often best on the dropping tide). Needs a huge swell to work.
13 Horton Sheltered southeast-facing beachbreak, needs a big swell to work. Best from mid to high tide.
14 Llangennith Three-mile stretch of consistant west-facing beachbreak.

Exposed spot, best on a clean swell with winds from the east quadrant. Ideal for beginners. Works on all tides up to neap high.

Also in this area:
Spot 'V' Left point-break over sand, offering long but slowish rides. Faces north, needs a huge swell, and only works on spring high tides. Not suitable for beginners. ✘ Rips.
Spots 'S', 'R' and 'Q' Cluster of remote southwest-facing reef breaks (a longish right, a hollow left, and a hollow right) which work on clean 3-6ft swells, around low tide only. They all need glassy conditions (or light northerlies) to be any good. Experts only. ✘✘ Rocks; rips.

Spot 'O' – a wedgy left somewhere in Dyfed.
Photo: Phil Holden

WALES

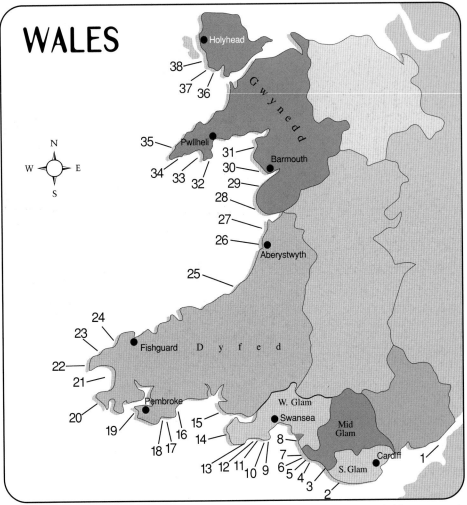

Holyhead

38
37 36

Gwynedd

35
Pwllheli
31
Barmouth
34 33 32
30
29
28
27
26
Aberystwyth

25

24
23
22
21

Fishguard   D y f e d

Pembroke
W. Glam
Swansea
15
Mid
Glam
16
14
20
19
8
7
18 17
6
Cardiff
13 12 11 10 9 5 4
1
S. Glam
3
2

N
W — E
S

DYFED

15 Pembrey Exposed southwest-facing beachbreak, best from mid to high tide. ✗ Rips.

16 Tenby, South Beach Southeast-facing beachbreak, needs a huge swells to work, but can offer hollow waves from mid to high-tide.

17 Manorbier Southwest-facing beachbreak which works as a right point at high tide, with waves breaking over sand-and-rocks. Needs a biggish swell, and light winds from the north quadrant ideally.

Great scenery with Norman castle overlooking the beach. ✗ Rips; rocks.

18 Freshwater East Sheltered southeast-facing beach which only works on huge swells, best around three-quarters tide.

19 Freshwater West Consistant southwest-facing bay with central beachbreak area, and various rocky breaks farther south. Exposed spot, needs a clean swell and winds from the east quadrant to be good. Works on all tides except high. Not suitable for beginners. ✗ Rocks; rips; quicksand at the northern end.

20 Marloes Sands, Westdale Bay
Pair of remote, southwest-facing
beachbreaks, best around low tide.
✘ Rocks.
21 Newgale Southwest-facing sand-
and-shingle beach, works from low
to mid-tide.
22 Whitesand Bay Consistant
west-facing beachbreak, works on all
tides. Good low-tide rights at the
northern end of the beach if the
sandbars are lined up. ✘ Rips when
over 4ft.
23 Abereiddy Remote west-facing
beachbreak which needs a big swell
to break. Works on all tides. Left-
hand reef at the southern end of the

beach is sometimes good at mid tide.
✘ Rocks.
24 Abermawr Another remote
west-facing beachbreak, Abermawr
needs a big swell to work, and only
breaks around low tide. Not suitable
for beginners.
25 Aberaeron Northwest-facing
spot a couple of miles north of the
town which can offer good lefts
breaking over cobbles on a big
southwest swell. Best around mid
tide. ✘ Rocks.
26 Aberystwyth harbour trap
Lefts breaking over a reef of rock
and mussel-beds, situated just north
of the harbour entrance. Faces west;

*Spot 'R' – a left
reef on the Gower
Peninsula.
Photo: Chris Power.*

Longboarder Chris Griffiths pulls into a Gower reef barrel.
Photo: Phil Holden

works from mid to high-tide. Advanced surfers only **✗✗** Rips; rocks; pollution.

27 Borth West-facing shingle beachbreak, works on all tides.

Also in this area:

Spot 'P' Right-hand boulder point with longish waves breaking over sand-and-rocks. Faces east and only breaks on the very biggest winter swells. Exposed spot, so only light westerly winds are any good. **✗** Rips; rocks.

Spot 'O' Secluded southeast-facing beachbreak which can offer good hollow wedgy waves on a big swell. A sheltered spot, it's best from mid to high-tide.

Spot 'N' Remote, sometimes inaccessible, right reef-point. When it's on, fast hollow waves break along the edge of a long finger of rock. Faces west, and only works from mid to high-tide. Dangerously shallow break for experts only. **✗✗** Rocks; rips.

Spot 'M' Rivermouth right-hander which breaks over sand. Long, fast

waves when it's on. Faces northwest and requires a huge swell to work; best around mid tide. **✗** Rips.

GWYNEDD

28 Tywyn Average southwest-facing beachbreak; best an hour after high tide. **✗** Rips when over 4ft; may occasionally be affected by sewage pollution.

29 Llwyngwril Left point-break over boulders. Faces north and needs a big swell to work, but can provide good long walls when it's on. Only works at high tide. Advanced surfers only. **✗✗** Rocks.

30 Barmouth Average west-facing beachbreak; works on all tides. **✗** Rips.

31 Llandanwg Northwest-facing spot with waves breaking over sand-and-boulders. Needs a big swell to work; best from mid to high-tide. Advanced surfers only. **✗** Rips; rocks.

32 Porth Ceiriad South-facing beach with good hollow waves when it's on; best around high tide.

33 Hell's Mouth (Porth Neigwl)

Four-mile-long bay which faces southwest. The most consistant spot in North Wales. Mostly beachbreak, best around mid tide. There's also a left at the southeast end which can be good at low tide, plus a short right which breaks over sand-and-rocks a few hundred yards farther along the beach (best around high tide). ✗ Rips when over 3ft; rocks in places.

34 Aberdaron South-facing beach, always smaller than it's neighbour Hell's Mouth but sometimes good around high tide.

35 Whistling Sands (Porth Oer) Northwest-facing beachbreak, needs a big swell to work. Best around high tide. ✗ Rips.

36 Aberffraw Southwest-facing beachbreak, rights sometimes good at high tide. Needs a big southwest swell.

37 Cable Bay Sheltered west-facing beachbreak, best from mid to high tide. ✗ Rips.

38 Rhosneigr Southwest-facing beach with rocky outcrops which works on all tides.

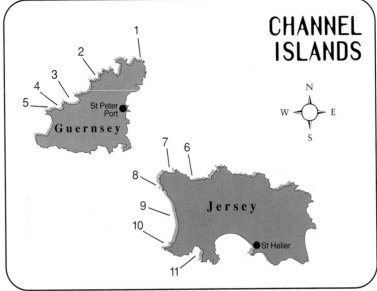

CHANNEL ISLANDS

Situated 15 miles from France's Cherbourg peninsula, the Channel Islands receive slightly less swell than Cornwall, mainly from the west. With a tidal range of up to 40ft, continuously shifting peaks and rip currents affect many of the breaks.

GUERNSEY

1 Fort Le Marchant Challenging left point-break situated at the northwestern tip of the island. It faces northeast, only works on huge swells, and only from low to mid-tide. Must be 6ft plus to break clear of the rocks. Dangerous spot for experts only. ✗✗ Rocks; rips.

2 Portinfer Northwest-facing spot with waves breaking over sand and rocks. Best on the dropping tide from mid to low-tide.

3 Vazon Bay Northwest-facing bay with an area of beachbreak (best from mid to three-quarters tide) towards the northern end; plus a central rocky area, **Vazon Reef**, with a right and a left breaking off either side (around high tide only). On big swells, the right joins up with another peak to become a longer wave known as **T'Otherside** which breaks towards the southern end of the bay. ✗ Rocks; rips.

4 Dom Hue Offshore big-wave reef, 8-12', with rights best. The wave breaks as a big peak and has been compared to Guethary in France. Works only around high-tide. Very long paddle. Experts only. ✗✗ Rocks, rips.

5 Perelle Bay Northwest-facing rocky bay, with a fast right and a long left breaking either side of an area of rocks in the centre of the bay, some 300 yards out to sea. Being so exposed, the waves need glassy conditions (or light winds from the east quadrant) to be any good. Both waves only work around high tide. Advanced surfers only. ✗ Rocks; rips.

JERSEY

6 Greve de Lecq Small north-facing bay with hollow waves breaking over sand-and-rocks when it's on. Needs a huge swell to work; best around low tide.

7 Plemont Northwest-facing beachbreak, best around low-tide. Tends to close-out a lot, okay on the occasional northerly swell.

8 'Stinky Bay' Shallow left-hand reefbreak which can give fast and hollow waves around low tide. Southerly winds best. Advanced surfers only. ✘ Rocks.

9 St Ouen's Bay Five-mile stretch of consistant west-facing beachbreak, rocky in places. Various spots are surfed, among them: **Secrets**, towards the northern end, with longish low-tide rights breaking over sand-and-rocks; **the Watersplash**, a popular beachbreak (best around low tide) opposite the Watersplash Inn; and **Les Brayes**, towards the southern end, a sometimes punchy beachbreak, best on a dropping tide at around mid tide. ✘ Rocks in places; rips when over 4ft.

10 Petit Port Heavy west-facing right reef, 8-12ft; Jersey's big-wave spot. Needs a big clean swell, works from mid to high-tide only. Difficult access. Dangerous break for experts only. ✘✘ Rocks; rips.

11 St Brelade's Bay Sheltered south-facing beachbreak, needs a huge swell to work; best from low to mid-tide.

Jersey surfer Renny Gould tucks into a clean barrel at St Ouen's. Photo: Scotty.

SCOTLAND

THE NORTH SHORE

Pounded by swells from the Atlantic and Arctic oceans, Scotland's North Shore offers some of the most powerful surf in Europe. Despite the northerly latitude, sea temperatures here are relatively mild because of Gulf Stream currents; nevertheless, many surfers wear 5mm wetsuits throughout the summer and autumn.

1 Oldshoremore Southwest-facing beachbreak. Needs a biggish swell to work, best from mid to high-tide.

2 Sandwood Bay Remote northwest-facing beachbreak that works on all tides. Access is by a track from Blairmore, the last three miles of which have to be done on foot, through some very boggy terrain. ✖ Rocks in places; rips.

3 Balnakiel Bay West-facing beachbreak, works on all tides.

4 Durness (Sango Bay) Northeast-facing beachbreak, works on all tides.

5 Kyle of Tongue North-facing inlet with sandy beaches on either side that can sometimes have good waves when there's a huge swell running.

6 Torrisdale Bay North-facing beachbreak with occasionally good rights at the rivermouth at the eastern end. Needs a biggish swell to work; best from low to mid-tide. ✖ Quicksand, rips.

7 Farr Bay Northwest-facing beachbreak, works on all tides.

8 Armadale Bay Sheltered north-facing beachbreak, works on all tides.

9 Strathy Sheltered north-facing beachbreak, with rights breaking off the rocks at the eastern end at high tide. ✖ Rocks.

10 Melvich North-facing bay with cobblestone reef, next to the rivermouth giving good rights-and-lefts from mid to high-tide when it's on. Works from 3-6ft. Melvich village may be the best place to park as the road that leads to the beach is private. ✖ Rips, rocks.

11 Sandside Bay Good left reef-

break next to the harbour at the village of Fresgoe; faces northeast and needs a big swell to work. Situated across the bay from the Dounreay nuclear plant. Sandside works from mid to high-tide only; winds from the southwest or west blow offshore. Shallow break for experts only. ✗ Rocks.

12 Brimms Ness Cluster of three north-facing reef-breaks situated three miles west of Thurso. A remote, exposed spot, Brimms picks up any swell going, but is adversely affected by any winds other than from the south quadrant. **The Bowl** and **The Cove** are hollow right-handers which work from mid to high-tide. **The Point** is a low-tide left which wraps around the rocks at the eastern end. Heavy waves breaking over shallow rock ledges, for experts only. ✗✗ Rocks; rips.

13 Thurso harbour reef North-facing reef with rights-and- lefts;

A small clean wave breaks over the boulder reef at Melvich. Photo: Chris Power

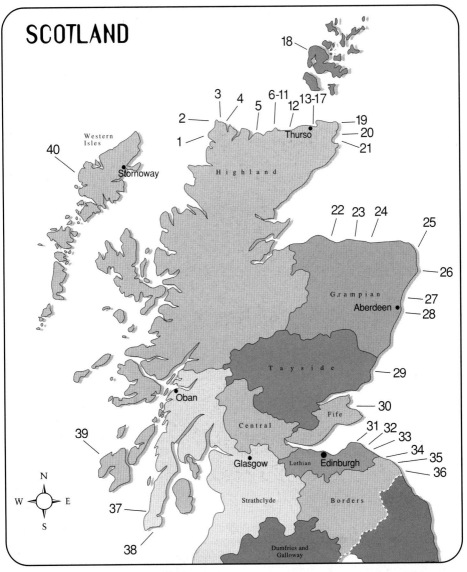

SCOTLAND

18

3
4
2
5 6-11
12 13-17
1 Thurso
19
20
21

Western
Isles

40

Stornoway

Highland

22 23 24
25

26

Grampian
Aberdeen
27
28

Tayside
29

Oban

30

Fife
31 32
33
34 35

Central

Glasgow
Lothian
Edinburgh
36

39

Strathclyde

Borders

N

W   E

S

37

38

Dumfries and
Galloway

needs a biggish swell to break, works on all tides. ✘ Rocks.

14 Thurso East Northwest-facing right reef-break, 4-15ft, situated a mile east of the town, opposite the castle. Excellent tubing wave when it's on. Best from low to mid-tide (good towards high tide if it's 6ft or bigger). Fast, heavy waves breaking over shallow rocks, for experts only. The brownish colour of the water is due to peat particles washed down the river, not pollution. ✘ Rocks.

15 Murkle Point Left reef-point; faces north and needs a biggish swell to work. Shallow rocky spot for experts only, best around mid tide. ✖ Rocks.

16 Dunnet Bay Northwest-facing beachbreak, works on all tides.

17 Point of Ness Right point at the northern end of Dunnet Bay. Faces southwest and works best on a westerly swell, from mid to high-tide. Winds from the east blow offshore, but there's reasonable protection from northerlies. ✖ Rocks.

18 Orkney Islands Although most of the west-facing coasts of these remote islands are inaccessible because of tall cliffs, a few good reef-break spots are known. The rocks here are the same flat flagstones as those of the Thurso area.

19 Skirza Harbour Good left point-break over boulders, situated four miles south of John O'Groats. Faces southeast, and works on a southeast or huge north swell. Works on all tides, becoming hollower the lower the tide (but dangerously shallow at low tide with rocks exposed). ✖ Rocks.

20 Sinclair's Bay Isolated east-facing beachbreak, works on all tides.

21 Ackergill Pair of right reef-points, 4-8ft, situated just east of the village. Both spots face north, and work on a big southeast or huge north swell, from low to mid tide only. ✖ Rocks; rips.

GRAMPIAN

22 Lossiemouth Average northeast-facing beachbreak, works on all tides.

23 Sandend Bay North-facing beachbreak, with lefts breaking off the harbour around mid tide.

24 Banff Small coast town with two main spots. In front of the pavilion at the eastern end of **Byondie Bay** is a right reef-point, 4-10ft, which can give long rides on a clean northerly swell, from mid to high tide. To the east, the rivermouth offers lefts breaking over sand-and-rocks (works on all tides). ✘ Rocks; rips.

25 Fraserburgh Northeast-facing bay with two main spots. **The Broch** is a beachbreak which works as a left point on biggish swells from mid to high-tide. **Philorth**, farther east down the beach, picks up more swell, and also works best from mid to high-tide. Past sewage pollution problems should be eradicated by improvements due to be completed during 1995.

26 Cruden Bay East-facing beachbreak which works on southeast (and big north) swells. Best from mid to high tide. ✘ Rips.

27 Balmedie Long stretch of southeast-facing beachbreak, works on all tides.

28 Aberdeen Two spots are surfed here. **Aberdeen Beach** is a long east-facing stretch of beachbreak with numerous groynes; it works on all tides, best on a clean south swell around low tide. **Nigg Bay**, just south of the city, has a boulder reef which can offer good rights on a big north swell, best from low to mid tide. ✘ Cross-shore rips; rocks at Nigg Bay.

29 Lunan Bay East-facing beachbreak; works on all tides.

30 St Andrews Northeast-facing beachbreaks at West Sands and the harbour; both work on all tides,

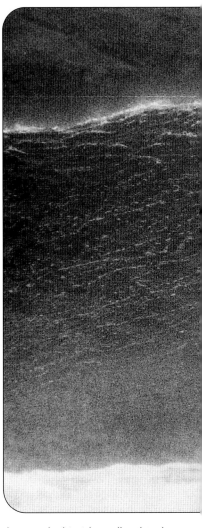

but need a biggish swell to break.

LOTHIAN AND BORDERS

31 North Berwick North-facing left-hand reef at the town end of East Bay. Works on a biggish northerly swell, from mid to high-tide. Advanced surfers only. ✘ Rips; rocks.

32 Dunbar (Belhaven Bay)

Northeast-facing beachbreak, best from mid to high-tide. ✗ Rips.

33 White Sands Left reef situated near the cement works three miles east of Dunbar. Faces northeast; should only be surfed as the tide pushes in, from low to mid tide. ✗✗ Bad rips on outgoing tides as the inlet empties.

34 Pease Bay North-facing beachbreak (works on all tides), with boulder reef at the eastern end which works from mid to high-tide. Best on a north swell, but also works on a big southeast swell. ✗ Rocks in places.

35 Coldingham Bay Sheltered east-facing beachbreak with a reef at the southern end; works from mid to high-tide. ✗ Rocks in places.

36 Eyemouth Northeast-facing

Neil Harris carves a turn on a big wall at Thurso East. Photo: Andy Bennetts / Camera Visions

A hollow beachbreak at Cliff, on the Isle of Lewis. Photo: Ed Legge.

beachbreak, works from low to mid tide only. ✖ Rips, pollution.

KINTYRE

Although most of the west coast of Scotland receives little swell because of the blocking effect of the Hebrides, the long promontory of Kintyre does pick up northwest swells.

37 Macrihanish, Westport Northwest-facing stretch of beachbreak, best from mid to high-tide. ✖ Rips.

38 Southend (Dunaverty Bay) South-facing beachbreak, needs a big swell to work. Reef near the headland, best around mid tide. ✖ Rocks.

INNER HEBRIDES

39 Islay Situated 15 miles west of Kintyre, Islay picks up swell from the west and northwest. **Saligo** and **Machir** are west-facing beachbreaks with powerful waves, best from low to mid-tide. **Laggan Bay**, next to the airstrip, faces southwest and needs a biggish swell to break; it works on all tides. ✖✖ Rips.

OUTER HEBRIDES

40 Lewis, North & South Uist The west coasts of these remote islands pick up any Atlantic swell going and have dozens of beachbreaks. A few of these – such as **Valtos, Cliff** and **Bragar** – have been surfed, but those who've explored here urge caution because of the strong rips and powerful shorebreaks that may be encountered. Both Lewis and the Uists have roads running along their western coasts. ✖✖ Rips; rocks in places.

THE EAST COAST

THE NORTHEAST

The waters of the North Sea are the coldest, and in places the dirtiest, around Britain. However, the rewards for the surfers who live here are a number of excellent spots, which work on north swells (or on the occasional shortlived southeast swell).

1 Bamburgh Northeast-facing beachbreak, works on all tides. Great scenery with Gothic castle overlooking the beach.

2 Blyth Sheltered east-facing beachbreak adjacent to south wall of harbour. Needs a big swell to work; best from mid to high-tide.

3 Hartley Reef Heavy northeast-facing reef, 4-10ft, with rights-and-lefts. Situated just north of St Mary's lighthouse. Needs a clean northerly swell plus light winds from the west quadrant to be good; works only from mid to high-tide. Experts only. ✖ Rocks.

4 Tynemouth Two main spots. **Longsands** is an east-facing beachbreak (with rocks in places), best from mid to three-quarters-tide. **King Edward's Bay** ('Eddies') is a sheltered east-facing beachbreak, best from low to mid-tide. ✖ Poor water quality.

5 The Black Middens Heavy left reef-break situated just inside the north breakwater at the mouth of the River Tyne. Needs a huge swell; only works around low tide. Northwesterlies blow offshore. Experts only. ✖✖ Bad pollution; rocks; rips.

6 South Shields Northeast-facing beachbreak with slowish waves, best around mid tide. ✖ Pollution.

7 Hartlepool Coastal town with three main spots. **Steetley Pier** is a northeast-facing beachbreak, best around low tide. **The Point,** situated near the shipwreck on the headland, is a gnarly right reef-break (experts only), 4-10ft, which works around high tide only. **Seaton,** to the south, is an east-facing beachbreak, best around high tide. ✖ Pollution; rocks at The Point.

8 The Gare Fast right-hander

breaking over boulders inside the south breakwater at the mouth of the River Tees (the break is about 300 yards upstream from the lighthouse). Works on big east or southeast swells, from low to mid-tide. Advanced surfers only. **XX** Bad pollution; rocks; rips.

9 Redcar North-facing beachbreak, works on all tides. **X** Pollution.

10 Saltburn North-facing spot with beachbreak waves either side of the pier (best around high tide); and a right reef-point, **Saltburn Point**, at

Long left-handers peel in at The Harbour, one of three quality breaks to be found at Spot L.
Photo: The Gill

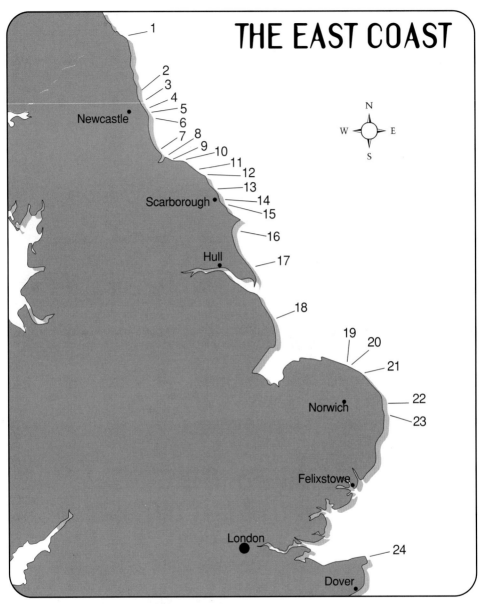

THE EAST COAST

1

2
3
4
5
6
7 8
9 10
11
12
13
14
15

16

17

18

19 20
21
22
23

24

Newcastle

Scarborough

Hull

Norwich

Felixstowe

London

Dover

N
W E
S

the eastern end of the beach (needs a good northerly swell, best around mid tide). ✖ Pollution; rocks at the Point.

11 Skinningrove Just south of the village, **Hummersea Scar** is a north-facing right reef, which

works from low to mid-tide. ✖ Rocks; poor water quality.

12 Runswick Bay Sheltered bay which turns on when the other spots in the area are being pounded by a big north swell. The best wave here is the right-hand

reef in front of the yacht house, which faces northeast and works from low to mid-tide. ✖ Rips, rocks.

13 Sandsend Bay Northeast-facing bay near Whitby with a long stretch of beachbreak (best from low to three-quarters-tide); and a good left reef-break, **Caves**, at the northern end of the beach under the cliffs, which works around mid tide. ✖ Rocks.

14 Scarborough Seaside town with breaks either side of the headland. **North Bay** faces north and offers waves breaking over sand-and-rocks; it works from low to mid-tide only. **South Bay** is an east-facing beachbreak which needs a big swell to work, best from low to mid-tide. ✖ Rocks.

15 Cayton Bay Popular northeast-facing bay with three

main spots. **The Point** (Osgodby Point), at the northern end, is a gnarly left reef-point (experts only) which works on big swells, around high tide only. **The Pumphouse**, inside the Point, is a mid to high-tide spot with waves breaking over sand-and-rocks. **Bunkers**, at the southern end, is a beachbreak best from mid to high-tide. ✖ Rocks in places; rips when over 4ft.

A clean four-foot swell marches in at Saltburn Pier Photo: Gary Rogers

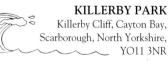

10 GOOD REASONS TO JOIN THE BRITISH SURFING ASSOCIATION

1 **Third Party Public Liability Insurance: FREE** Insurance cover of up to £2,000,000 in case you accidentally injure someone while you are surfing; applies worldwide.

2 **Surf News: FREE.** The British Surfing Association's newsletter*, delivered to your door, six times a year. Packed with news, features and photos.

3 **BSA Yearbook: FREE.** Includes rules and regulations covering surf contests in Britain; life-saving procedures for emergencies; hints for judges; lists of past contest winners; surf clubs around the country; and more.

4 **Information and advice: FREE.** Whatever you want to know about any aspect of surfing in Britain (or abroad) we're here to help.

5 **Save money on surfing lessons.** BSA members pay less for lessons at the National Surfing Centre, Fistral Beach, Newquay.

6 **Surf contests.** The BSA organises the most prestigious amateur contests in the country: the British Nationals, the British Cup, the British Student Championships, the British Schools Championships, and the British Inter-Club Championships.

7 **Save money on equipment and clothing.** BSA members get discounts of up to 15% off equipment and clothing from the dozens of shops across the country who participate in our discount scheme.

8 **Coaching and judging courses.** The BSA regularly runs coaching accreditation courses (for surfers wishing to teach surfing lessons to the public), and judging courses (for surfers wishing to judge at amateur or pro-am contests), at very reasonable rates.

9 **Save money on magazine subscriptions.** BSA members pay less for subscriptions to CARVE Surfing Magazine and THREESIXTY Bodyboarding Magazine.

10 **Represent your country.** If you're good enough, you might even make it into the British Team, and get to travel to the World Championships in South Africa in 1996!

For further details contact the BSA: BSA Champions Yard, Penzance, Cornwall TR18 2TA. Tel 01736 60250.

16 Filey Bay Average-quality east-facing beachbreak, with some shelter from northerly winds at the northern end. ✘ Rips when over 4ft.

Also in this area:
Spot 'L' Cluster of three good left reef-breaks situated near a village with a seafaring historical connection. The lefts on either side of the harbour are good but **The Cove**, to the south, is the best spot. All three face north and work on a clean northerly swell, from low to mid-tide. Fast, hollow waves breaking over shallow rock ledges, for advanced surfers only. ✘ Rocks, pollution.

HUMBERSIDE, LINCOLNSHIRE AND EAST ANGLIA

17 Withernsea Average-quality shingle beachbreak, with numerous groynes built to impede longshore drift. Faces northeast, best from low to mid tide.
18 Sutton-on-Sea Unremarkable beachbreak, probably the best spot in the area though. Faces northeast, best around high tide.
19 East Runton North-facing spot with waves breaking over sand-and-rocks, best from mid to high-tide; probably East Anglia's best break. Rarely works during the summer. ✘ Sharp flints, cross-shore rips.
20 Cromer Average north-facing beachbreak, works on all tides. ✘ Pollution.
21 Walcott Average beachbreak;

faces northeast, best around low tide.
22 Gorleston-on-Sea Average east-facing beachbreak, with sheltered spot next to the harbour wall. Needs a big north swell to work. ✘ Cross-shore rips.
23 Lowestoft Average east-facing shingle beachbreak with numerous groynes; needs a big north swell to work, best around low tide. ✘ Cross-shore rips.

EAST KENT

24 Joss Bay Northeast-facing spot with central area of average-quality beachbreak, plus various rocky chalk reef breaks; generally best around high tide. Needs a huge north swell charging down the North Sea to work. ✘ Rips, rocks in places.

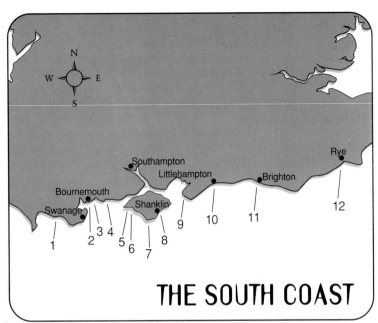

THE SOUTH COAST

The South Coast is an inconsistant area for waves, since only the very biggest southwest groundswells travel far up the Channel. Many of the breaks described below are more commonly surfed on short-lived storm swells from the southwest, south, or east.

DORSET

1 Kimmeridge Bay South-facing bay with shelving rock ledges. Doesn't work very often: only good on a southwest groundswell, with glassy conditions or light northerlies. Three spots are surfed at Kimmeridge, all best on the dropping tide at around three-quarters tide. **Broad Bench** (at the western end of the bay) is a

shallow right reef-point, 3-8ft, with fast hollow waves when it's on, for advanced surfers only; unfortunately it's part of an MoD tank firing-range, and is strictly off-limits most weekdays. **The Bay** is a right reef-break, situated in the middle of the bay, only really surfed when the other spots are too big. **The Ledges** is a another reef with mainly slowish lefts at the eastern end of the bay. ✘ Rocks; rips; MoD firing range (Broad Bench); crumbling cliffs.

2 Bournemouth Pier, Boscombe Pier Popular south-facing beachbreak spots which work on all tides. Always crowded when there's a wave. ✘ Rips when over 4ft.

3 Southbourne Average south-facing beachbreak, works on all tides.

Winter waves at Bournemouth Pier.
Photo:
Chris Power

4 Highcliffe Average south-facing beachbreak, works on all tides up to three-quarters tide.

Also in this area:
Spot 'K' Reef break with short rights-and-lefts situated next to a famous stone breakwater. Needs a huge southwest swell and winds from the north quadrant to be any good. Works from low to mid tide only. Shallow break for advanced surfers only. ✖ Rocks.

ISLE OF WIGHT

5 Freshwater Bay Right-hand point situated towards the western end of the island. Doesn't work often but can offer good waves breaking over rocks when it's on. Faces south. Needs a big southwest groundswell plus light winds from the north quadrant to be any good. Works from low to mid tide only. Advanced surfers only. ✖ Rocks.

6 Compton Bay Probably the most consistant spot on the Isle of Wight, Compton is a southwest-facing beachbreak which is best around three-quarters tide.

7 Niton South-facing spot situated on the southern tip of the island which can occasionally offer good rights breaking over sand-and-rocks. Needs a big southwest swell plus light northerlies to be any good, works around three-quarters tide only. Advanced surfers only. ✖ Rocks.

SHORE WATERSPORTS

SHOP AND MAIL ORDER CATALOGUE

SURF • WINDSURF • BODYBOARD • SAIL • WATERSKI • CANOE

ISSUE 7 SPRING/SUMMER 1995

24 HOUR
MAIL ORDER
SERVICE

01243 672313

INDEX
2/3	GUL Wetsuits
4/5	SOLA Wetsuits
6/7	O'NEILL Wetsuits
	BODY GLOVE/
8/9	SHORE Wetsuits
10/11	BOOTS/REPAIR
12/13	GLOVES/DIVE
14/17	WINDSURF
18/21	SAIL
22/23	SURF
24/27	BODYBOARD
28/29	WATERSKI
30/31	CANOE
	CLOTHING
32/33	QUIKSILVER
34/35	O'NEILL
36/37	BODY GLOVE
38/39	MAMBO/RUSTY
40/41	TUCANO/SALTROCK
	HEADWORX
42	SUNGLASSES
43	TIMBERLAND
44	REEF/CONVERSE
45	WALLETS
46	ORDER FORM
47	WATCHES
48	

Chartered Trust
INSTANT CREDIT
AVAILABLE

STORES AT
Shore Road
EAST WITTERING W Sussex
Chichester 01243 672315
PO20 8DZ 01243 673759
FAX: 01243 673759

Northney Marina
HAYLING ISLAND
Hampshire
PO11 0NH
01705 467334

NEW 48 PAGE SPRING/SUMMER BROCHURE OUT NOW!
MASSIVE RANGE - DON'T MISS OUT

1

8 Shanklin (Hope Beach) East-facing beachbreak which needs a massive southwest swell or an east swell to work. Best around three-quarters tide. ✘ Cross-shore rips, pollution.

HAMPSHIRE, SUSSEX, AND THE SOUTH COAST OF KENT

9 West Wittering, East Wittering Southwest-facing stretch of sand-and-shingle beachbreak with numerous groynes. Needs a huge southwest swell or an east swell to work, plus northerly winds ideally. Best around high tide. ✘ Cross-shore rips.

10 Littlehampton Wedgy peak next to the breakwater at the mouth of the River Arun. Faces south and works best around high tide. Experienced surfers only. ✘ Rips.

11 Brighton The shingle beaches along the seafront aren't too great for surfing (occasionally okay from low to mid tide), but there are a few chalk reef spots to the east which can offer some reasonable waves.

12 Hastings, Rye South-facing beachbreaks of average quality, best around high tide.

• *Joss Bay (on Kent's northeast coast) is described in chapter 12, The East Coast, on page 65.*

LIPSMACKIN'TUBECHARGIN'TAILSLIDIN'BEACHCRUISIN'SECTIONFLOATIN'WAVECARVIN'BEERSWILLIN'CUTTYGOUGIN'NOTWORKIN'JUSTSURFIN' carve

British Surfing Association

producing
champions
since 1966

British Surfing Association

the winner's choice

carve

SURFING MAGAZINE

POWER

BIGGER
HARDER
HEAVIER

AVAILABLE FROM ALL
GOOD SURF SHOPS AND
NEWSAGENTS

GLOSSARY

Aerial An explosive manoeuvre where the surfer launches himself into the air, off the top of the wave.

Barrel A tubular section of a wave within which a surfer can find the meaning of life.

Backhand To ride with your back to the wave.

Beachbreak Waves that break over a sandy bottom, ideal for beginners.

Bottom turn Having dropping down the face of the wave, this is the first turn a surfer uses to set up his next move.

Closeout A wave which breaks along its length all at once, without peeling. Also known as a straight-hander.

CARVE A cool surf mag. Also a powerful turn that throws up loads of spray.

Cutback A manoeuvre performed on the shoulder of the wave that turns the surfer back toward the pocket.

Duck dive The method used by a surfer to push his or her board under an oncoming wave while paddling out.

Drop in When a surfer takes off on a wave that someone else is already riding; a serious breach of surfing etiquette. Remember: the surfer nearest the curl has right of way.

Ding A hole in your surfboard. Often the result of dropping in!

Forehand To ride facing the wave.

Floater A manoeuvre where the surfer rides over the breaking section of the wave and free-falls down the wave's curtain.

Filthy Extremely good.

Glassy Clean, smooth surf conditions when there is no wind.

Gnarly An evil mutha of a wave, intent on destruction., evil conditions.

Goofyfoot A surfer who rides right-foot-forward.

Going off! When the waves are really good, or someone's ripping.

Grommet A young surfer with no respect for his elders, usually in need of some severe discipline!

Groundswell A swell caused by a low pressure system quite a way offshore.

Gun A long, narrow surfboard designed for riding big waves.

Impact zone The area where the waves break.

Kook An idiot who has no idea what he's doing.

Left-hander A wave that breaks towards the left as seen from the line-up.

Line up The area where waves jack up before they break, where surfers wait.

Local Someone who surfs a spot regularly, and enjoys moaning on and on about crowds.

Mal Traditional style surfboard around nine feet in length. Hang ten dude!

Natural foot A surfer who rides left-foot-forward.

Nailed To get hammered by the lip of a big wave.

Offshore When the wind blows from the land to the sea, holding up the

waves. The ideal wind for surfing.

Onshore The exact opposite. Time to head down the pub!

Over the falls The worst kind of wipe-out, when you get dragged down stuck in the lip of the wave.

Pit A hollow, jacking section of a wave. Pull in!

Pointbreak A rock headland around which waves peel, either to the left or right.

Pumping When the surf is going off. Head for the beach!

Pocket The part of the wave just in front of the curl, where it's steepest.

Quiver A selection of surfboards to suit different conditions.

Rails The edges of a surfboard.

Reefbreak A wave that breaks out to sea, over a slab of rock or coral. Not suitable for beginners.

Rip A dangerous current that can pull you out to sea. If you get caught in one, don't panic, but paddle across it to where the waves are breaking.

Righthander A wave that breaks towards the right, as seen from the line-up.

Rhino chaser A really big board designed for charging huge waves.

Rocker The bottom curve along the length of a surfboard.

Set A group of larger waves which come in periodically.

Shorebreak Where waves break close to the sand at a steep beach.

Shoulder The sloping unbroken part of the wave ahead of the pocket.

Soup The whitewater where a wave has just broken. Also a nice hot liquid to be consumed in large quantities after a winter session.

Tube The same as a barrel.

Zoo A badly crowded line-up.

Hawaii's Shawn Briley about to experience a hefty closeout at Backdoor. Photo: Mike Searle

EMERGENCIES

The following is only intended as a guide to emergency action. Every surfer should do a basic course in water safety, rescue skills and resuscitation. The question you should ask yourself is this: if your best mate was in serious trouble would you know what to do to help? Contact your nearest branch of the Royal Life Saving Society or Surf Life Saving Society for details.

WATER RESCUE PROCEDURE

If you are on the beach or in the water, and you see or hear someone in distress, you may need to perform a water rescue.

1. Assess the situation. Do not risk your own life if you are not sufficiently experienced in the prevailing conditions. Establish what needs to be done, and what assistance is needed.

2. Send for help. Phone, or tell someone else to phone the nearest lifeguard hut, or the coastguard (dial 999). Get the help of other surfers, especially locals who are likely to be more confident in rough conditions.

3. If you are absolutely confident that you can assist the person in trouble without putting your own life at risk, then act calmly but quickly. Always use a rescue aid, such as your surfboard or a Peterson Tube.

4. The person in trouble may well be distressed or shocked. Talk to him as you approach; try to sound confident, even if you are nervous. When you are two metres away, pass your board (or rescue aid) to him. Do not allow him to grab you.

5. Keep the person calm, and reassured. If you know help is on its way, it may be best to wait for assistance.

6. If no help is coming, or the situation requires immediate action, place the person on your board and paddle in to shore, lying on top of him. Be aware of approaching waves, and keep the patient secure on the board. An unconscious casualty must be brought back to shore as quickly as possible; if he is not breathing, start mouth-to-nose respiration (see below).

8. Once back on the beach give the appropriate aftercare.

THE ABC OF RESUSCITATION

A – Airway Open the airway by lying the person flat on their back, lifting their jaw and tilting the head back. Carefully remove any obstruction from the mouth.

B – Breathing Check the person is breathing. Look to see if his chest is rising and falling; listen and feel for his breath against your cheek.

C – Circulation Check the pulse. Find the pulse by placing your fingers against the side of the Adam's apple (voice box) and pressing gently down.

* **If there is a pulse and the casualty is breathing**, put him in the recovery position (on his side with the head tilted back to keep the airway open).

* **If there is a pulse but no breathing**, start mouth-to-mouth

(or mouth-to-nose if at sea) respiration.

a. Pinch the casualty's nostrils firmly shut and open the airway.

b. Take a deep breath and seal your lips around the casualty's lips. Blow into the mouth watching the chest rise. Let the chest fall completely. Continue at about 10 breaths per minute, checking the pulse after every 10 breaths.

c. Once the casualty starts breathing, put him in the recovery position.

* If there is no pulse and no breathing, start mouth-to-mouth respiration and chest compression.

a. Give two breaths of mouth-to-mouth.

b. Place the heel of your hand two fingers' breadth above the junction of the rib margin and breastbone. Place your other hand on top and interlock your hands.

c. Keeping your arms straight, press down by no more than two inches. Then relax the pressure to allow the heart to refill. Continue compressions at a rate of 80 per minute, but stopping every 15 compressions to give two breaths of mouth-to-mouth.

d. Keep checking the pulse. Stop chest compression as soon as a pulse returns.

NEVER start chest compression if the heart is beating.

DO NOT give up until medical assistance arrives.

BLEEDING

Raise the part of the body which is bleeding (if possible), and use a clean pad to apply direct external pressure to the site of the wound. Seek medical help immediately.

A casualty is stretchered off the beach at Pipeline, Hawaii. Thanks to the immediate assistance he received, he made a full recovery. Photo: Mike Searle.

INDEX

Clean offshore waves at Constantine Bay, Cornwall. Photo: Chris Power.

generations of

experience

in extreme

wetsuit

technology

"if the glove fits... wear it"

BODY GLOVE WETSUITS HEAD OFFICE: OCEAN QUAY, RICHMOND WALK, STONEHOUSE, PLYMOUTH, DEVON PL1 4QA.
TEL: 01752 551510 FAX: 01752 606890

Y GLOVE CLOTHING CORE BRANDS LTD. HEAD OFFICE: THE OLD BEAMS, THREE HOUSEHOLDS, CHALFONT ST. GILES, BUCKS HP8 4LJ.
TEL: 01494 873934 FAX: 01494 871279

Made in the U.K.

exacting standards , Gul wetsu

have been used since 1967

D u r a b i l i t

dedicated surfers in the cold

hostile surf conditions of

North Atlantic and North

P e r f o r m a n c

around Britain and the rest

Europe.

With extreme weat

F l e x i b i l i t

conditions and year round w.

temperatures ranging fr

41° - 61° we know how to m

W e t s u i t

Durable, Flexible and W

Wetsuits.

We have to .

Taylor
KNOX

Russell
WINTER

Renan
ROCHA

Todd
PRESTAGE

Ad Design : S.E.A.Studio   Photo : Alex Williams

w e t s u i

Head Office : Gul International Ltd , Walker Lines , Bodmin , Cornwall , England PL31 1EZ Tel : 01208 72382 Fax : 01208 75

Argentina Hardwind Comercio 56-22287130 Benelux Interfield 31-171834411 Brazil Bloody Runners 55-112646785 Canaries SD Importaciones 922-176189 Chile Hardwind 56-22287130 Cyprus Force Eight 357-53544266 Czech TTI Therm 42-69
Denmark Surf 7 Ski 45-42862586 Finland Bri Fin 358-5118164 Greece Glaridis 301-4113163 Hong Kong Pro Shop 852-7236816 Iceland Islenka 354-126488 Japan ASG Inc. 81-48-226-0121 Norway Lilleby 47-33314626 Portugal Simoes 351-148
South Africa S&N Enterprises 27-41552480 Spain Eurodisa 34-34515058 Sweden Delva 46-40436080 USA Murrays Marine 180-56848393 UK Gul International Ltd 44-208 72382